U.S. National Parks

Jenna Winterberg

Publishing Credits

Rachelle Cracchiolo, M.S.Ed., *Publisher*
Conni Medina, M.A.Ed., *Managing Editor*
Nika Fabienke, Ed.D., *Series Developer*
June Kikuchi, *Content Director*
John Leach, *Assistant Editor*
Kevin Pham, *Graphic Designer*

TIME For Kids and the TIME For Kids logo are registered trademarks of TIME Inc. Used under license.

Image Credits: p.10 Library of Congress [LC-DIG-ggbain-21286]; p.11 (top) Brian Bruner, (bottom) Everett Collection Inc/Alamy Stock Photo; p.12 Pictorial Press Ltd/Alamy Stock Photo; p.13 Aurora Photos/Alamy Stock Photo; pp.18–19 Interfoto/Alamy Stock Photo; p.19 (left) Courtesy National Park Service, NPS History Collection, HFCA #HPC-001064, photographer Cecil W. Stoughton; p.24 National Park Service Photo by William H. Jackson; all other images from iStock and/or Shutterstock.

Library of Congress Cataloging-in-Publication Data

Names: Winterberg, Jenna, author.
Title: Parks for All : U.S. National Parks / Jenna Winterberg.
Description: Huntington Beach, CA : Teacher Created Materials, 2017. | Includes index.
Identifiers: LCCN 2017017371 (print) | LCCN 2017018902 (ebook) | ISBN 9781425853532 (eBook) | ISBN 9781425849795 (pbk.)
Subjects: LCSH: National parks and reserves--United States--Juvenile literature.
Classification: LCC E160 (ebook) | LCC E160 .W56 2017 (print) | DDC 363.6/8--dc23
LC record available at https://lccn.loc.gov/2017017371

Teacher Created Materials
5301 Oceanus Drive
Huntington Beach, CA 92649-1030
http://www.tcmpub.com

ISBN 978-1-4258-4979-5
© 2018 Teacher Created Materials, Inc.
Made in China
Nordica.072017.CA21700822

Table of Contents

Don't Change a Thing

President Theodore Roosevelt was in awe of the Grand Canyon. "Leave it as it is," he said. He wanted to keep it "as one of the great sights which every American, if he can travel at all, should see."

He worked to preserve natural resources, and many other people have followed in his footsteps. They want canyons, forests, glaciers, sand dunes, and more set aside for protection. These people save wildlife. They are called **preservationists**.

Thanks to them, we have national parks. Through these parks, we can explore the past, play in the present, and protect the future.

bighorn sheep

Showdown in Arizona

Locals didn't want the Grand Canyon to become a national park. It would restrict their use of the land and water. Only an act of Congress can create a national park, so Roosevelt made it a national **monument** to protect the area. It became a national park 11 years later.

Man vs. Nature

The country was going through big changes at the end of the nineteenth century. Settlers came west, where land was cheap. Trees were chopped down to build towns. Wild grasses were cleared to build farms. People hunted bison and birds.

Americans at that time saw this as progress. They felt nature should be tamed. A new railroad connected big cities across the country. It also made remote places more accessible. Developers had their eyes on these places.

Some of these lands had scenic and striking landscapes. Congress acted to preserve these natural treasures for everyone. By 1900, it had named six national parks.

19th Century Parks

1872	1875	1890

Yellowstone National Park

Mackinac National Park (became a state park in 1895)

Sequoia National Park

Lower Yellowstone Falls, in Wyoming, is 308 feet (94 meters) high.

Parks Galore

In 1872, Yellowstone became the first national park. Now, there are 59. The National Park Service (NPS) also oversees landmarks and seashores. In all, there are 413 NPS sites in the United States.

1890	1890	1899

General Grant National Park (became part of Kings Canyon National Park in 1940)

Yosemite National Park

Mount Rainier National Park

Lawless Land

Yellowstone became a national park at a time when most public land was being sold off. But in the beginning, no one thought about its upkeep or about protecting its wildlife. There was nothing to prevent **vandals** from harming the land. People stayed in the park. They hunted wildlife and cut down trees.

One man oversaw Yellowstone. But he was unpaid and had another job that kept him busy. He stepped inside the park only twice in five years! The men who held the job after him were not any more effective. Congress refused to give money to protect the park. So 14 years after Yellowstone became a national park, the U.S. Army took charge. Soldiers stood guard and patrolled the parks, but the only way for them to punish lawbreakers was to **evict** them.

hot spring pool in Yellowstone National Park, Wyoming

Save the Bison

In 1902, few bison were left in Yellowstone due to illegal hunting. When a report spread about a **poacher** in the park, the public took note. They pushed Congress to give the army a way to enforce rules. Today, there are over 5,000 bison in Yellowstone.

THINK LINK

> Who benefits from the **establishment** of national parks? Who is harmed by it?

> Why do we need laws to protect natural spaces?

> Can parks be preserved and still be open to people?

Buffalo Soldiers

In the nineteenth century, the army gave some African American men a rare chance to lead in a time when bias against them was strong. An all-black unit served in Yosemite, Sequoia, and General Grant national parks. American Indians called these men "buffalo soldiers" for their fierce look.

Colonel Charles Young

The most well-known buffalo soldier was Charles Young. He took charge of Sequoia National Park in 1903 and became the park's superintendent. A son of enslaved parents, the West Point grad was the first black man to rise to this rank.

Honoring Young

Young was the first black graduate of his high school in Ohio. He moved there with his family not long after his father escaped slavery. His childhood home in Wilberforce, Ohio, is now a national park site. It's called the Charles Young Buffalo Soldiers National Monument.

High Honors

Buffalo soldiers built a trail to the Giant Forest in Sequoia National Park. The trail is still in use. The "Colonel Young Tree" is a popular landmark.

COLONEL YOUNG TREE

Park Patrol

The buffalo soldiers patrolled the parks in the summer. They traveled from their post in San Francisco. It took them 13 days to reach Yosemite and 16 days to Sequoia. By car, it now takes around four hours for each leg of the trip.

Leaving a Legacy

Many trails in California parks are named after John Muir. He loved nature and fought to protect it. He spread his ideas through writing. He wrote more than 300 articles and 12 books about the wild. He reached millions of readers.

President Roosevelt was a fan of Muir's. He invited Muir to camp with him in Yosemite. "I want to drop politics absolutely for four days and just be out in the open with you," the president said. By day, the men hiked. They saw meadows, glaciers, mountains, and waterfalls. By night, they talked by the campfire. The trip had an impact on the president.

Father of the National Parks

Muir (right) influenced officials, including Roosevelt (left). Muir knew that only the government could save the wild lands for the future. He fought tirelessly for the cause—and is much of the reason our parks exist.

Roosevelt's Parks

While in office, Roosevelt signed five acts from Congress to create parks: Crater Lake, Wind Cave, Sullys Hill (now a national game preserve), Mesa Verde, and Platt (now part of Chickasaw National Recreation Area). By the end of his time in office, there were 11 national parks.

John Muir Trail, Yosemite, California

A Man of Action

In his youth, Roosevelt worked on a ranch. During this time, he wrote a book about hunting. The editor of a journal called *Forest and Stream* wrote a bad review of it. When Roosevelt went to confront him, the two found they had a lot in common. Both men believed that wildlife would go extinct without help. They called attention to their cause through articles and letters.

Roosevelt kept up this fight as president. But his power had limits. Only Congress could name national parks. So he asked to be able to create monuments. This way, he could protect places without Congress's approval. The Antiquities Act of 1906 gave him that right. During his eight years in office, he named 18 monuments!

Forest Service

In 1905, Roosevelt started the U.S. Forest Service. Its goal was to protect nature. Today, the U.S. Forest Service cares for 154 national forests and 20 grasslands.

FOREST SER
U S
DEPARTMENT OF AGRICL

Ahead of His Time

"What will happen when our forests are gone, when the coal, the iron, the oil, and the gas are exhausted?" Roosevelt said in a speech at the White House in 1908. His words are still fitting.

Montezuma Castle National Monument, in Arizona, was named by President Roosevelt.

The Way of the Wild

Wildlife Welfare

The Endangered Species Act was passed in 1973. Since then, officials have kept a list of animals (and plants) at risk of dying out.

215

national park sites that are home to endangered species

$12 million

amount spent on species recovery programs in 2010

5,000+

species of mammals, birds, reptiles, amphibians, and fish in the parks

1,652

plants and animals in the United States listed as threatened or endangered in 2017

Threatened and Endangered Species in the National Parks (2011)

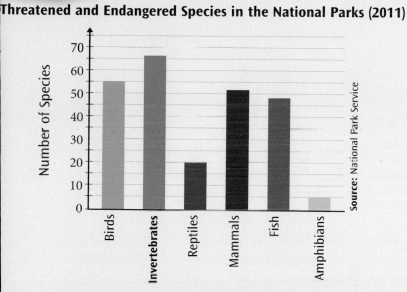

Number of Species (y-axis): 0, 10, 20, 30, 40, 50, 60, 70

Animal Species (x-axis): Birds, Invertebrates, Reptiles, Mammals, Fish, Amphibians

Source: National Park Service

Where to See Endangered...

Red Wolves

Alligator River National Wildlife Refuge, North Carolina

Florida Panthers

Big Cypress National Preserve, Florida

Black-Footed Ferrets

Badlands National Park, South Dakota

California Condors

Pinnacles National Park, California

The Parks Expand

The parks were run as separate sites until 1916, when Congress started the National Park Service (NPS). Most parks were in the West at that time. Fewer settlers in the West meant more open space. The land there was owned by the government, so it came at no cost.

But these parks were remote and wild. To succeed, the NPS needed to attract more visitors. This required support. The NPS wanted to create more parks and increase access to all parks. **Engineers** made parks more accessible. States in the East began to set aside land that could become parks and monuments. More sites were added to the NPS.

Sharing the Wealth

Patrons put up their own money to help protect park lands. Businessman John D. Rockefeller Jr. spent millions on parks in the East. Stephen T. Mather, the first director of the NPS, paid to expand parks in the West.

Park Women

Women did not have many roles in national parks at first. Six women had paid jobs in the NPS by 1930. But they were denied the **ranger** job—and could not wear pants!—for 40 years. Things have changed. Since 2000, two directors of the NPS have been women.

Grand Canyon

Parks of a New Nature

President Franklin D. Roosevelt made a big change in 1933. He put U.S. battlefields, forts, and memorials in the hands of the NPS. Then, historic sites were added to the lands the NPS managed.

Next, national seashores, **recreation** areas, and lakeshores were put under the control of the NPS. These areas, along with parkways and waterways, were part of a new trend. They were meant to be used by large numbers of people. These new parks all had nature at their hearts. But they were not the same as the wild preserves of the past.

Setting a Record

Former president Barack Obama is credited with protecting the most land and water. He reserved over 550 million acres for the public. He set a new record with his monument count, too. The 29 sites that he reserved honor a wide range of groups.

Lincoln Memorial

STOP! THINK...

Most Visited NPS Sites in 2015
Yellowstone is an **iconic** park—but it isn't among the most visited. Only one national park is in the top five most visited NPS sites. Why do you think other sites attract more visitors?

> Blue Ridge Parkway, North Carolina and Virginia

> Golden Gate National Recreation Area, California

> Great Smoky Mountains National Park, North Carolina and Tennessee

> Lincoln Memorial, Washington, DC

> Lake Mead National Recreation Area, Arizona and Nevada

QUIET
RESPECT
PLEASE

Building Balance

How can parks preserve nature and give access to visitors? The answer lies in trails and roads. Trails guide people. They offer a safe way to explore NPS sites. And they protect the **flora** and **fauna** off the paths.

At first, roads were built only when they were needed. But when cars became more popular, this changed. Many people wanted to see nature from the comfort of their cars. The roads that **wind** (WYND) through the parks were carefully planned. They have to make a major impact on viewers but a minor one on the landscapes.

For example, in Zion National Park, in Utah, cars are not allowed during busy months. Instead, clean, quiet buses take visitors on the park's canyon roads.

Bring Nature to the People

Not everyone has a car—or time to take long trips. National trails were set up near cities to bring nature within reach. Now, there are 30 trails, from the scenic Pacific Crest to the historic Trail of Tears.

A Boost from the Depression

The Great Depression of the 1930s was a time of hunger and need. Paid work was hard to find. The Civilian Conservation Corps was formed in 1933 to put young men to work in the parks. From trails to toilets, these crews built much of what we now use in the parks.

road built in Bryce Canyon National Park, Utah

For the Record

Big and small, high and low, the National Parks go to extremes!

today

1871

Oldest Park

Yellowstone National Park, Wyoming, Montana, Idaho
Established: 1872
Size: 2.2 million acres (8,991 square kilometers)
This park has looked the same since it was established. Photos from 100 years ago show the same beautiful landscapes.

Sizing Things Up

Largest: Wrangell-St. Elias National Park, Alaska
Size: 13.2 million acres (53,419 square kilometers)
The park is six times the size of Yellowstone.

Smallest: Hot Springs National Park, Arkansas
Size: 5,549 acres (22 square kilometers)
It includes areas where people can use the hot springs to relax.
Yellowstone is 400 times the size of this park.

High and Low

Highest: Denali Mountain, 20,310 feet (6,190 meters)
Denali National Park, Alaska
This mountain is the highest point in the national parks—and in North America!

sea level

Lowest: Badwater Basin, 282 feet (86 meters) below sea level
Death Valley National Park, California
This is the lowest point in North America. It is the hottest, too!

A Plan for the Future

The history of U.S. national parks has had as many twists and turns as a scenic road. These sites were first set up to protect land and water. Now, they preserve wildlife and culture.

Popular NPS Sites

Mount Rainier

Yellowstone

Mount Rushmore

Redwood National Park

Great Sand Dunes

Grand Canyon

Carlsbad Caverns

Waco Mammoth

Park visits have hit new highs, but the NPS wants to reach even more people. Many programs aim to attract visitors, including "Every Kid in a Park." This program offers free visits for fourth graders. The parks belong to all of us—the goal is for all of us to enjoy them.

Glossary

engineers—builders or designers of machines or public use items like roads and bridges

establishment—the act of founding

evict—to remove from a place, usually with force

fauna—animals

flora—plants

iconic—symbolic; stands for something else

invertebrates—animals without a spine

monument—site of historical or cultural interest

patrons—people who support a cause, a person, or a group, typically with money

poacher—someone whose hunting or fishing activity is against the law

preservationists—people who protect something, often used to refer to nature

ranger—keeper of a park, forest, or other protected land

recreation—leisure activity taken on so one can relax and enjoy

vandals—people who damage or destroy property

wind—twist and turn

Index

Check It Out!

Books

National Geographic. 2016. *Guide to National Parks of the United States*. National Geographic.

Runte, Alfred. 2010. *National Parks: The American Experience*. Taylor Trade Publishing.

Stetson, Lee. 2013. *The Wild Muir: Twenty-Two of John Muir's Greatest Adventures*. Yoscmite Conservancy.

Videos

Abraham, F. Murray, and Rodney Schumacher. *National Parks Collection*. National Geographic.

Burns, Ken. *The National Parks: America's Best Idea*. PBS.

National Park Service. *Watching Wildlife: Webcams*. www.nps.gov/subjects/ watchingwildlife/webcams.htm.

Websites

National Park Service. www.nps.gov.

PBS. *The National Parks: America's Best Idea*. www.pbs.org/nationalparks.

Try It!

Many voices spoke up to protect natural, wildlife, and cultural sites. Now, it's your turn to be a preservationist!

- 🍃 Select what you want to preserve. It could be a historic site, park, animal, or something else.

- 🍃 Come up with reasons why your choice is worth saving.

- 🍃 Write a letter or speech to convince others to join you in your preservation project. Explain the strengths of your plan and how they outweigh the weaknesses.

- 🍃 Draw a picture or take a photo to go with your letter or to display during your speech. The picture should show the value of the place or thing you'd like to preserve. Make sure the meaning is clear.

About the Author

Jenna Winterberg has worked on car catalogs, novels, fashion magazines, and more. Science, travel, and the outdoors are some of her favorite subjects. The national park sites she likes best are Zion National Park and Dinosaur National Monument. She lives in Los Angeles, where she hikes, camps, and climbs any chance she gets.